Cambridge Primary Path 4

Grammar and Writing Workbook

Catherine Zgouras

CAMBRIDGE
UNIVERSITY PRESS

Contents

1 How do we express feelings?

Grammar: Interrupted Past

We all have bad days, right? Well yesterday, I had the worst day EVER. It started before I was even awake. <u>While I was sleeping soundly in bed, my little brother slammed his bedroom door.</u> It startled me. At first, I was scared. I calmed down after I realized what it was. Nice way to wake up. Later, while I was taking a shower, the hot water ran out. I was sooooo annoyed. Next, while I was making cereal for breakfast, I dropped the bowl on the floor. The cereal went everywhere. What a mess! Mom was NOT happy. I had to clean it all up, which made me late. Then, guess what? While I was running to the bus stop, I tripped and fell. And while I was picking up my books, the bus suddenly drove off. I wanted to stamp my feet because I was sooooo mad. This made me late for school. When I finally got there, I realized that my homework was still on my desk at home. I was starting to cry when the teacher announced that the homework wasn't due until tomorrow! What a relief!

1 **Read the blog post. How did Emily feel?**

When she woke up: _____ When the hot water ran out: _____
When she heard the teacher's announcement: _____

2 **Read again and complete the sentences. Then, underline the sentences in the text that use the interrupted past.**

  a While Emily _____, the hot water _____.

  b While she _____ breakfast, she _____ the bowl of cereal.

  c While she _____ for the bus, she _____ and _____.

Grammar: Interrupted Past

We use the past progressive and the past simple to show that a longer action in the past was interrupted by a shorter one.

While I was having breakfast, I spilled milk everywhere.

Mom called Dad while he was washing the dishes.

Remember!

We always use past simple for the action that interrupts the longer one.

While Maria was watching TV, the telephone rang.

The tablet stopped working while I was downloading some music on it.

3 Underline the action that was in progress. Circle the action that interrupted the action in progress.

a Matt (fell) while he <u>was dancing.</u>

b While Rosie was sleeping, her phone rang.

c The computer stopped working while I was surfing the Internet.

d While Penny was dancing, she broke her arm.

e He burned his hand while he was cooking.

4 Read, choose, and circle the correct words.

a While he **walked /** (**was walking**) down the street, he saw his friend.

b Paolo found his old phone while he **was looking / looked** for his wallet.

c While Lucy was studying in her room, she **heard / was hearing** a noise in the kitchen.

d I **was losing / lost** my keys while I was running in the park.

e The baby started crying while she **played / was playing**.

5 Complete the sentences with the past simple or past progressive.

a While Sharon __was walking__ **(walk)** her dog, it ___started___ **(start)** barking at the mail carrier.

b While I _____ **(chat)** with my friend, my cell phone _____ **(run)** out of battery.

c Jenny _____ **(break)** the mirror while she _____ **(clean)** her bedroom.

d While I _____ **(ride)** my bike, I _____ **(get)** a flat tire.

6 Read and write sentences using the interrupted past.

a A bee / sting / Jackie / while / we work / in the garden.

A bee stung Jackie while we
were working in the garden.

c While / Mom / watch TV / she / fall asleep.

_____

_____

b A dog / chase / Pete / while / he walk / to school.

_____

_____

d While / the students / take a test / the teacher / sneeze.

_____

_____

7 Write two things you were doing when someone or something interrupted you.

While I was sleeping, my brother turned on the radio.

_____

_____

ASK ANTHONY

Q: Hello, Anthony. I'm nervous about my next history test because I don't understand anything! I feel so miserable! – Pedro

A: Pedro, you should ask your teachers for help. They will explain things to you in more detail. If you don't ask for help, you won't do well on your tests.

Q: Hey, Anthony! I always feel tired in the morning, but I can't stop watching TV late in the evening. – Tanya.

A: Hi, Tanya. If you search for the shows on the Internet, you will find they are available to watch on your computer. If you watch them on the weekend, you will get more sleep and feel better!

Q: Hi, Anthony. My friend always asks me to do her homework. If I tell the teacher, she won't be my friend anymore! – Tim

A: Hello, Tim. Talk to your friend. Explain how you feel. If she doesn't want to be your friend after that, you will know that she isn't a real friend.

① **Read the *Ask Anthony* advice column again. Mark ✓ the correct sentence.**

   a   Anothony has no friends. ☐

   b   Anthony gives advice. ☐

   c   Anthony asks for advice. ☐

② **Read the column again and circle *if*, *will*, and *won't*. Then, complete the sentences.**

   Anthony says:

   a   If you _____search_____ for the shows on the Internet, you _____will find_____ they are available to watch on your computer.

   b   If you _____ for help, you _____ well on your tests.

   c   If she _____ to be your friend after that, you _____ that she isn't a real friend.

Grammar: First Conditional

We use the first conditional to talk about things that might happen in the future.

> **If it rains, we won't go to the stadium.**
>
> **They will stay home if there is a good movie on TV.**

Remember!

a Always use a comma if the first conditional sentence starts with *If*.

> **If it's nice on the weekend, we will go to the beach.**

b Use the present simple after *if*. Use *will / won't* in the clause that shows the result.

> **If we go to the beach, we will have a picnic.**

3 **Choose the correct words to complete the sentences.**

a   will have / goes
   If John _____goes_____ out tonight, he _____will have_____ pizza.

b   is / will get
   Sandy _____ a haircut if her hair salon _____ open today.

c   will get / study
   The students _____ good grades if they _____ hard.

d   won't be / leave
   If we _____ early, we _____ late for the show.

e   won't know / don't listen

   If they _____, they _____ what to do next.

4 **Match.**

1   She won't be angry   a   he will tell you about the party.

2   If John sees you,   b   we will buy another video game.

3   We won't be happy   c   if you ask her first.

4   Sarah will ride her bike to school   d   if our team loses the game.

5   If we have enough money,   e   if it's sunny.

5 Look and write sentences.

a If they / water the plant / it grow.

If they water the plant, it will grow.

b You / be healthy / if you / eat healthy food.

_____

c If Tom / not go to bed early / he / be tired / in the morning.

_____

d If we / not pick up our trash / our parks / be dirty.

_____

6 Complete the sentences with the correct form of the verbs in parentheses.

a If I _____*meet*_____ (meet) a famous person, I _____*will ask*_____ (ask) for an autograph.

b I _____ (feel sick) if I _____ (eat) too much chocolate.

c The singer _____ (not sing) if he _____ (be) too tired.

d If George _____ (drive) fast, he _____ (have) an accident.

e If they _____ (not practice), they _____ (lose) the game tomorrow.

7 Complete to make true sentences about yourself.

a If I get up late, _____*I will miss the school bus*_____.

b Mom and Dad will be happy if _____.

c If I don't do my homework, _____.

Adjectives

We use adjectives to describe people, feelings, and things.
To describe feelings or emotions, we use adjectives that end in *-ed*.

> **Juan felt excited when he heard about the summer vacation.**

> **Mom was tired after working all day.**

To describe things like movies, books, or events, we use adjectives that end in *-ing*.

> **The book about outer space was interesting.**

> **The movie was boring.**

(1) Read and circle.

a   Gabriel was **tired** / **tiring** after playing tennis all day.

b   We had a good time at the soccer game because it was very **excited** / **exciting**.

c   I felt **frustrated** / **frustrating** because the test was very difficult.

d   Pedro was **embarrassed** / **embarrassing** when he forgot his lines during the play.

e   Thunder and lightning can be very **frightening** / **frightened**.

(2) Read and complete the words with *-ed* or *-ing*.

a   The teacher was annoy_____*ed*_____ because the children were making too much noise.

b   Mary told us some very frighten_____ ghost stories.

c   I enjoy doing yoga—it's very relax_____.

d   I couldn't understand the story because it was confus_____.

e   We were exhaust_____ after walking up the steep hill.

1 READ Read the acrostic poems. What are the hidden words?

Every now and then,

e**X**citing and

spe**C**ial occasions make us laugh and

have fun unt**I**l

we are very **T**ired.

Then, w**E** fall asleep

and **D**ream about a happy tomorrow.

Stressed with **T**oo many things to do:

got up early **I**n the morning

didn't **R**est until

It was dark.

But could**N**'t sleep because

the next day it all started a**G**ain.

2 EXPLORE Read the poems again. Circle the adjectives. How many lines are there in each poem? Why?

_____

_____

_____

3 **PLAN** Think about your acrostic poem. What is your hidden word? How many letters does it have? Which adjectives can you use? Complete the graphic organizer.

Hidden Word	Number of Letters	Adjectives

4 **WRITE** Write your acrostic poem. Use the graphic organizer to help you.

_____

_____

_____

_____

_____

_____

_____

_____

_____

_____

CHECK

Did you ...
- spell your hidden word correctly? ☐
- add a line for each letter? ☐
- include adjectives? ☐

Read the email and write the missing words. Write one word on each line.

Dear Ben,

I am very excited today. Yesterday it was my sister's birthday, but we had so

Example many problems organizing it. While Mom _____was_____ baking the cake, the oven stopped working! We didn't know what to do. Dad went to a bakery to buy a cake, but it was closed. Then, Grandma had a great idea! She opened

1 ten packages of cookies and three jars of strawberry jam. She _____ a cake with the cookies. It looked like a pyramid. My sister loved her cake and

2 took a photo of it. She sent it to her friend _____ China. Then, her friend in China showed it to her father. He's a chef in a big restaurant. He thinks

3 Grandma's cake is better _____ his. He asked my grandmother go to

4 China and make the same cake! My grandmother _____ taking me and my sister with her!

5 So, if I don't answer your phone call, I _____ be on a plane flying to China!

Love,

Daniel

2

What can space exploration teach us?

Grammar: Reflexive Pronouns: *myself, yourself, himself, herself, itself, yourselves, ourselves, themselves*

CZI: Hey, Mike! Did you go to the Science Fair last week?

MTa: Hi, Carl! Yes, I did. It was cool.

CZI: Did you see the model of the solar system? I made it (myself.)

MTa: Really? It was amazing. Did you see the rocket? The one with pencils and cardboard?

CZI: Yes, it was very creative.

MTa: My friends, Bill and Tony, made it themselves. They cut out cardboard, used colored paper for the jet steam, and glued it all together.

CZI: How smart! What did you make?

MTa: Did you see the Moon Machine?

CZI: Yes, I did! It won first prize! Was that yours?

MTa: Yes, it was. Rami and I made it ourselves. I designed it, and Rami found all the information about how to put it together by himself.

CZI: That's awesome! What did you win?

MTa: We each won a book about the moon.

1 Read the dialogue. Whose project was very creative?

2 Read the dialogue again. Circle the reflexive pronouns in the text. Then, match.

1	Carl	a	He found the information about how to build the Moon Machine himself.
2	Bill and Tony	b	We made the Moon Machine ourselves.
3	Rami and Mike	c	I made the mobile myself.
4	Rami	d	They made the rocket themselves.

We use reflexive pronouns when the subject and object of the verb are the same.

myself	ourselves
yourself	yourselves
himself / herself / itself	themselves

Dina made the robot herself.

They hurt themselves when they fell off their bikes.

Tip!

We can also use **by** before reflexive pronouns.

Harry solved the problem by himself.

Marianne found the clues to the puzzle by herself.

Spelling Rule

yourself ⟶ yourselves

3 **Read and circle the correct words.**

a   The children wore knee pads to protect **themselves** / **ourselves**.

b   Please help **myself** / **yourselves** and take as much food as you like.

c   I cut **myself** / **itself** when I was making a sandwich.

d   The dog barked at **itself** / **ourselves** when it looked in the mirror.

e   He can do the project **itself** / **himself**.

4 **Read and match.**

1   _____We_____ painted the picture ourselves.

2   _____ makes these cookies herself.

3   Did the radio switch _____ off again?

4   They keep _____ fit by jogging in the park.

5   I always talk to _____ when I'm trying to find an answer to a problem.

a   itself

b   myself

c   We

d   She

e   themselves

5 Read and complete the sentences with the correct reflexive pronouns.

Hi Amir!

Hope you are well. Guess what? My friends and I won the science competition!

We made two robots 1 ___ourselves___. It wasn't very easy. There were five members in my group. Jenny and Tara found all the materials 2 _____. Then, Pete taught 3 _____ all about programming and showed us. Manal worked on designing the robot by 4 _____, and then she showed it to us. I put the robot together 5 _____ late at night. Then, we programmed it, painted it, and started working with it. The robot talks to 6 _____, and we can't make it stop! The teacher thought it was funny!

What did you make for the science competition?

Talk to you soon,

Alice

send

6 Read and complete the sentences with reflexive pronouns.

Ellen made the scarf
by ___herself___.

Harry can dress
_____ even though
he's only three!

Tina and Mark are
teaching _____
how to play the guitar.

I fixed the bike
_____.

Dad and I painted
the walls _____.

SPACE FACTS

Saturn

Mars

• Saturn has a lot of gas, so it is less dense than the other planets. If you put an ocean on Saturn, it would float!

• The Moon's south pole is colder than the South Pole on Earth—it's minus 283 degrees Celsius. That is because the sun never shines on the moon's south pole.

• Space is quieter than Earth because there is no atmosphere in space. Sound can't travel, but astronauts communicate with each other using radio waves that can travel through space!

• A volcano on Mars is bigger than Mount Everest. It is still active. Because Mars has a lot of volcanoes and mountains, scientists believe that it is more volcanic than Earth.

• Outer planets have more extreme weather than Earth. Jupiter, Saturn, and Uranus have very strong winds, but Neptune, a dwarf planet, has winds up to 2,000 kilometers per hour!

1 **Read the text. Mark ✓ the correct sentence.**

   a Earth can float in the ocean. ☐

   b There are no active volcanoes on Mars. ☐

   c You can communicate in space with radio waves. ☐

2 **Read the text again and circle the comparatives that end in *-er*. Then, complete the sentences.**

   1 Saturn is ___less dense___ than the other planets.

   2 The Moon's south pole is _____ the South Pole on Earth.

   3 Jupiter, Saturn, and Uranus have _____ weather than Earth.

Grammar: Comparatives with *-er*, *more*, *less*, and *than*

Comparative adjectives compare one person or thing with another. We form the comparative with *-er* and *than*.

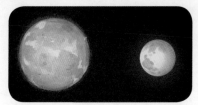

The sun is bigger than the moon.

We can also use *more* or *less* and *than* to compare two people or things.

The new car is more expensive than the old car.
The old car is less expensive than the new car.

Spelling Rule

pretty ⟶ prettier
happy ⟶ happier
big ⟶ bigger

3 **Read and complete the sentences.**

a Jane thinks drama is ___more interesting than___ music. **(interest)**

b New computers work _____ old ones. **(fast)**

c Some snakes are _____ spiders. **(poisonous)**

d Space shuttles are _____ cars. **(heavy)**

e A baby is _____ an adult. **(weak)**

4 **Write sentences using comparatives with *-er*, *more*, *less*, and *than*.**

a Jane / tall / Sarah.

   Jane is taller than Sarah.

b A tablet / cheap / a phone.

   _____

c A TV / expensive / a radio.

   _____

d Towns / noisy / cities.

   _____

5 Read and complete the sentences.

a   My brother is braver than me.

   I am _____*less brave*_____ than my brother.

b   My sister was more unhappy than I was.

   I was _____ my sister.

c   The book was less difficult to understand than the video.

   The video was _____ the book.

d   The movie theater was less crowded than the restaurant.

   The restaurant was _____ the movie theater.

e   The pizza was more delicious than the burger.

   The burger was _____ the pizza.

6 Look at the pictures and complete the sentences using *-er*, *more*, *less*, and *than*.

Mount Everest is
____*higher than*____
Mount Olympus. **(high)**

A monkey is
_____
a fish. **(intelligent)**

A city is
_____
a town. **(peaceful)**

7 Make true sentences using comparatives and the words in the box.

> funny   tall   exciting

a   _____ is more interesting than _____ .

b   _____ is more difficult than _____ .

c   _____

d   _____

e   _____

Definite and Indefinite Articles

We use indefinite articles (*a*/*an*) when we are talking about something for the first time. We use *an* with words that begin with *a*, *e*, *i*, *o*, *u*, and the silent letter *h*.

The children saw a **photo of** an **astronaut in the museum.**

We visited a **museum** an **hour ago.**

We can also use indefinite articles when we want to refer to something that isn't specific.

There was an **old spaceship in the museum, too.**

We use the definite article (*the*) when we want to refer to something specific. We also use it with the names of mountain ranges, rivers, seas, oceans, and groups of islands or stars.

The **spaceship in the museum was very old.**

The **photo of** the **astronaut on the moon was amazing.**

---

1 **Read and complete the sentences.**

> a   an   the

a   There was _____ video about space travel on the Internet.

b   Sarah made _____ nice poster showing all _____ planets in space.

c   _____ river near our home is very dirty.

2 **Read and circle the correct word to complete each sentence.**

1   **The / A** solar system was formed about 4.6 billion years ago.

2   **An / The** asteroid is a small rocky object in outer space.

3   **A / The** meteor is smaller than **an / the** asteroid.

_____1_____ January 23

_____ This morning we left home at 7:30 a.m. We drove to the city to visit the Planetarium. It was awesome!

We had a guide, and he explained how the solar system was formed and what stars, asteroids, and meteors are. He also gave us information about the planets in the solar system. We took a short break in the café.

Then, we went into the main theater. We saw a movie in 3D! It was like being in the International Space Station, or ISS. We could see what Earth looks like from space: we could see the clouds and the oceans. We orbited Earth really fast, but not as fast as the real ISS. The ISS orbits Earth every 90 minutes—that's about 16 times in one day! We also saw space junk. These are parts of space stations that fall off after being in space for many years. Space junk can stay in space for decades and then might fall back to Earth.

_____ In the afternoon, we visited the Space Museum. We saw an amazing photo of an astronaut in space and an old rocket. The rocket was very big. It went to space twenty years ago.

_____ In the evening, we stayed in our hotel and talked about our great day. Tomorrow, we are visiting the Science Museum. I can't wait!

1 **READ** **Read the journal entry. What did Tony see at the Planetarium?**

_____

_____

_____

_____

2 **EXPLORE** **Where are these things in the journal entry? Read and write the correct number next to each section.**

1 the date

2 what Tony did in the afternoon

3 what Tony did in the evening

4 what Tony did in the morning

3 **PLAN** Think about an interesting day you had. What did you do? Where did you go? What did you see? Complete the graphic organizer.

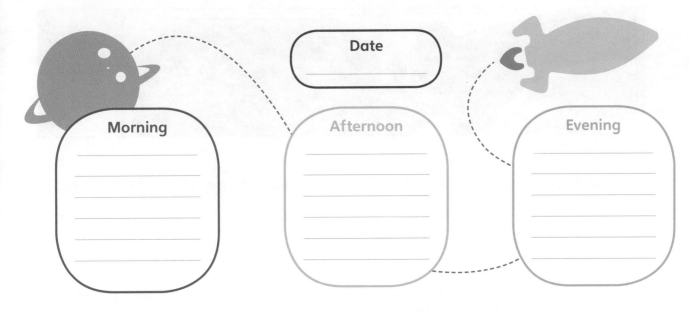

Date
_____

Morning
_____
_____
_____
_____

Afternoon
_____
_____
_____
_____
_____

Evening
_____
_____
_____
_____

4 **WRITE** Write your journal entry. Use the graphic organizer to help you.

_____

_____

_____

_____

_____

_____

_____

_____

_____

_____

CHECK

Did you ...

- write the date? ☐
- write in first person? ☐
- write where you went and what you did? ☐
- use articles correctly? ☐

Read the text. Choose the correct words and write them on the lines.

Space Satellites

Example The Moon is _a_ natural satellite. That means that nature made it. There are also

1   many human-made satellites _____ space. We send satellites to space

2   so we can learn more about it. They collect information about _____ planets, the Earth and Moon, oceans, and the weather. They send the

3   information back to the space stations. They _____ us make phone calls, watch TV shows, and listen to radio stations from all around the world.

4   They also send pictures of space _____ Earth. In 1957, Russia sent the first satellite to space. It was small and round and had four

5   antennas. Today, satellites are _____ than Russia's first satellite. They

6   _____ computers, batteries, and special machines that help them move

7   in space. They move in space on their own and make power _____. You

8   _____ see some satellites without a telescope because they are very

9   low in space. The _____ important satellite is the International Space

10   Station. People _____ in it and collect information about space. They help us understand what living in space is like.

Example	an	a	the
1	in	of	next
2	a	the	they
3	helping	helped	help
4	to	in	at
5	big	bigger	biggest
6	are having	has	have
7	yourself	ourselves	themselves
8	do	can	are
9	most	more	than
10	worked	works	work

3 Is technology good or bad?

Grammar: Present Perfect Questions (*yes/no*)

Advantages and Disadvantages of Technology in the Classroom

Technology has changed over time. We asked some students about technology in the classroom and what they think of it.

Q: Have you ever used the Internet in the classroom?

Yes, I have. I think it's very useful because I can find a lot of information very quickly. – Julia

Q: Have you ever looked for information in a library?

Yes, but it's frustrating because you have to find the books, and that can take a long time. There is also a problem with the Internet, though. Sometimes the information is wrong, so you always have to check where it comes from. – Kim

Q: Have you ever had a class on your computer?

No, I haven't. I think all classes should use computers or tablets instead of books. That will save paper because our books will be in the computer. – Yuri

Q: Has your computer ever broken down?

Yes, it has! One time, I lost all my notes, so that is a big disadvantage. – Lee

1 Read the text. Who lost all their project notes?

2 Read the text again. Complete the questions. Then, ask and answer them with a partner.

1 _____Have you ever used_____
   the Internet in the classroom?

2 _____
   for information in a library?

3 _____
   a class on your computer?

4 _____
   down?

We use the present perfect to ask people about past experiences when we are not sure exactly when the events happened. We usually use *ever* with these questions.

Have you ever **visited** a space station?

Has your mom ever been **upset with you?**

Have you ever **met** a famous person?

Remember!

We usually answer these questions using short forms.

> **Have you** ever **swum in a lake?**
> Yes, I have. / No, I haven't.
> **Has your brother** ever been **to Japan?**
> Yes, he has. / No, he hasn't.

③ **Read and circle the correct words.**

a (**Have**) / **Has** you ever made a blog?

b **Have / Has** Liam ever written a song?

c **Have / Has** Ellen and Mindy ever played volleyball?

d **Have / Has** they ever worked in a factory?

e **Have / Has** she ever visited Australia?

④ **Read and complete the sentences.**

a _____Has_____ Gina ever _____built_____ a snowman? **(build)**

b _____ the children ever _____ in a tent? **(sleep)**

c _____ Anna ever _____ virtual reality games? **(play)**

d _____ Dan and Tony ever _____ about their future? **(think)**

e _____ she ever _____ to buy a tablet? **(want)**

f _____ you ever _____ money in the street? **(find)**

5 Look at the pictures and make sentences using the present perfect and *ever*.

a (you / win / a race)

_____Have you ever won a race?_____

b (Eric and Sam / play / in a band)

_____

c (they / live / in a cold country)

_____

d (Tanya / move / to a new house)

_____

e (you / watch / a scary movie)

_____

6 Look at the table. Make questions and answers.

Nala	George and Eva	Michael	Tina	Claire and Frank
go skiing ✓	play the piano ✗	fly a kite ✓	bake a cake ✓	drive a car ✗

a _____Has Nala ever gone_____ skiing?

Yes, _____she has_____ .

b _____ the piano?

No, _____ .

c _____ a kite?

_____ .

d _____ a cake?

_____ .

e _____ a car?

_____ .

7 Answer the questions about yourself and a friend.

a Have you ever walked in the rain?

_____

b Have you ever had sushi?

_____

c Has your friend ever created a vlog?

_____

What did you use to do when you were younger?

I used to play computer games for three hours a day. My eyes used to hurt a lot. Now, I only play computer games an hour a day, and then I play outside with my friends. I feel better and healthier. – Sam

In my family, we used to look at our phones all the time. We didn't use to talk to each other, and we didn't use to spend time with each other. Now we put our phones away all evening. We play games and talk about our day. It feels good to talk to my family more often. – Anita

My brother and I used to waste a lot of time surfing the Internet. We didn't use to go outside. We used to be tired all the time, too. One day, we decided to time ourselves and only play on the computer for an hour. We had so much more time to do other things, like visit friends and listen to music! – Kelly

1 **Read the text. Do the children feel better or worse now?**

2 **Read the text again and underline all examples of *used to* and *didn't use to*. Then, complete the sentences.**

a I _____ used to play _____ computer games for three hours a day. – Sam

b We _____ at our phones all the time. We didn't
_____ to each other. – Anita

c We _____ outside. – Kelly

Grammar: *Used to / didn't use to*

We use *used to* and *didn't use to* to talk about things we did in the past that we don't do anymore.

Kate used to have long hair.

He didn't use to like vegetables, but now he does.

Did he use to walk to work? Yes, he did. Now he rides a bike.

Spelling

We form the affirmative with *used to*. However, we form the negative and interrogative with *use to*.

3) Complete the sentences.

a Ahmet _____used to like_____ tennis. **(like / ✓)**

b Tavo _____ a big breakfast. **(have / ✓)**

c Ana _____ her homework in the library. **(do / ✗)**

d _____ the boys _____ soccer in the park? **(play / ?)**

e Pete _____ comics. **(read / ✓)**

f Dina and Jesi _____ to rock music. **(listen / ✗)**

4) Read and match.

1 Jane used to take the bus to school,   a but now they live in a city.

2 We used to play in the park,   b but now they are best friends.

3 Omar didn't use to talk to Wendy,   c but now she walks.

4 They used to live in a small town,   d but now I love it.

5 Zahara used to play the guitar,   e but now we play in the backyard.

6 I didn't use to like pasta,   f but now she plays the trumpet.

5 **Unscramble to make sentences.**

a used to / they / at the stars / look / at night

They used to look at the stars at night.

b Amir / noisy / didn't use to / be

_____

c work / used to / the computer / well

_____

d did they / play sports / use to / at school

_____

e Zoe and Paul / didn't use / their grandparents / every day / to call

_____

6 **Look at the pictures. Then, complete the questions and answer them.**

a _____ James _____ climb trees?

No, he didn't. He used to climb mountains.

b _____ they _____ surf?

_____

c _____ she _____ sing in a rock group?

_____ in a choir.

7 **Make true sentences about yourself.**

a I didn't use to _____.

b I used to _____.

c _____

Prepositions Following Adjectives

We use prepositions, such as *about*, *with*, or *at* after some adjectives.
There is no rule for these prepositions.

Young children are very curious about **the world around them.**
Jenny is happy with **her new computer.**
I was surprised at **how easy the test was!**

1 **Read and circle.**

a   Miguel is very excited **with /** **about** his summer vacation.

b   Helen was happy **with / to** her new bike.

c   Disneyland is famous **to / for** its amazing rides!

d   My sister is afraid **with / of** the dark.

e   Mom is worried **about / with** Dad because he's very late.

2 **Read and complete the sentences.**

> in   with   for   at   ~~of~~

a   Technophobia is when you are afraid _____of_____ technology.

b   Doug Engelbart is responsible _____ inventing the computer mouse.

c   Lucy was good _____ school, but she didn't go to college.

d   More people are interested _____ computer programming than any other job.

e   Social networking is more popular _____ younger people.

1 **READ** **Read the email. What is Hala interested in?**

| **To:** greg@ourmail.com |
| **From:** halaws@welcom.com |
| [1] **Re:** tech park trip |

[2] Hi Greg,

We went to the city tech park today. It was really cool. I'm really interested in technology and new inventions! We learned a lot about technology. I was surprised at how many things we use today that are part of technology: cell phones, tablets, laptops, and even microwave ovens! Microwave ovens have small computers in them that make them work.

I was very excited about the new inventions at the tech park. There were smart watches that find the mistakes you make while you are doing your homework! Can you imagine how much time that saves?

I am also curious about technology and garbage. Did you know that the United States is responsible for throwing away more than 200 million computers and gadgets a year? That's a lot of garbage for one country!

I was really happy with the trip. Tomorrow I have to give a presentation about what I learned. I made a poster. I'm really proud of it!

[3] Have you ever been to a tech park?

[4] Your friend,

Hala

send

2 **EXPLORE** **Read the email again. Write the numbers. Then, underline the adjectives and prepositions.**

The subject: _____1_____

The greeting and ending: _____ and _____

A question: _____

3 PLAN You are going to write an email about technology. Think about the subject. Then, complete the graphic organizer.

Where did you go? / What type of technology are you writing about?	
What did you see and do there? / What can it do?	
Question	

4 WRITE Write your email. Use the graphic organizer to help you.

_____

_____

_____

_____

_____

_____

_____

_____

_____

CHECK

Did you ...

- write the subject? ☐
- write a question? ☐

- write a greeting and an ending? ☐
- use adjectives with prepositions? ☐

Read the text. Choose the correct responses and write the letters on the lines.

Katy is asking Uncle Pete about what he used to do and what he has done in the past.

Example

 Katy: Did you use to have computers in the classroom?

 Pete: _____E_____

A	No, I haven't, but I want to visit Spain one day.
B	I always play basketball.
C	We used to play soccer and tennis.
D	I used to walk with my friends.
E	No, we didn't. We only had notebooks and textbooks. **(Example)**
F	My favorite subjects were science and math.
G	I had pasta and chicken.
H	Yes, I played once. It was fun.

Questions

1 **Katy:** How did you go to school?

 Pete: _____

2 **Katy:** What were your favorite subjects?

 Pete: _____

3 **Katy:** What games did you play after school?

 Pete: _____

4 **Katy:** Have you ever played computer games?

Pete: _____

5 **Katy:** Have you ever traveled to another country?

Pete: _____

4 How do we entertain ourselves?

Grammar: Present Perfect with *ever* and *never*

Sam: Hey, Niamh. Want to hang out this afternoon?

Niamh: Sure, Sam. What do you want to do?

Sam: Well, we can write something for my vlog and make a short video! Have you ever made one?

Niamh: No, I've never made a short video. But I've written blogs before. I don't really like doing it. Have you ever played Snakes and Ladders? It's an old board game. It's a lot of fun.

Sam: Yes, I have. But I didn't like it. I know! We can play with my virtual reality headset. Have you ever used one?

Niamh: Yes, I have! Great idea!

Sam: Cool! Have you ever played tennis with it? It's so much fun.

Niamh: No, I've never played tennis with a VR headset before. Let's do that!

Sam: Great! Come over in about an hour.

Niamh: OK!

1. **Read the dialogue. Has Niamh ever written a blog?**

2. **Read the dialogue again. Underline the present perfect sentences with *ever* in green and the present perfect sentences with *never* in blue. Then, complete the sentences below.**

   a **Sam:** Have you _____ever made_____ a short video?

   b **Niamh:** I've _____ a short video.

   c **Niamh:** Have you _____ Snakes and Ladders?

   d **Niamh:** I've _____ tennis with a VR headset before.

We form questions in the present perfect with *ever* to ask about things that have happened at any time in the past.

Have you ever played chess?

We use *never* to answer in the negative form.

Joe has never played chess.

Remember!

We place *never* after *have* or *has* but before the main verb.

I have never swum in a lake.   **He has never played tennis.**

---

3 **Read and choose the correct words.**

a   Jim has **ever / never** eaten sushi.

b   Has Gina **never / ever** bought a laptop?

c   Zoe and Paul have **never / ever** seen a real giraffe.

d   Have the children **ever / never** played in the park?

e   Has Jon **ever / never** read an adventure book?

4 **Read and complete the sentences with *ever* or *never*.**

a   Valeria has _____never_____ fought with her brother.

b   Has Beto _____ asked you for help?

c   They have _____ cleaned their bikes!

d   Have those girls _____ spoken to you?

e   My computer has _____ broken down.

5 **Look at the pictures. Make questions with *ever* and answers with *never*.**

a she / eat / spaghetti and ice cream / ?

 Has she ever eaten spaghetti and ice cream?
 She has never eaten spaghetti and ice cream.

b they / ice-skate / before / ?

_____

They have _____ .

c Diana / play / the piano / ?

_____

She _____ .

6 **Make questions with *ever*.**

a you / drive / a go-kart
 Have you ever driven a go-kart?

b your parents / take you / to Australia

_____

c your teacher / be upset / with you

_____

d your friends / cheat / on a test

_____

e you / try / windsurfing

_____

7 **Look at Activity 6 again. Then, write your own answers to the questions.**

a I've never driven a go-kart. _____

b _____

c _____

d _____

e _____

Hi Niki,

We just got back from our "adventure weekend." Dad planned it all, and it was a lot of fun. First, we visited an escape room. Have you ever been to one? It was great. They put us in a room, and we had to find all the clues to get out of it. There's an Escape Center in our town, too, but it hasn't opened yet. Maybe we can go when it does.

Then, we went paintballing—it was so much fun! I hit Mom and Dad eight times. They had so many different colors on them. We can do that, too, some day—it doesn't matter that I've already played it before. I want to play it again.

Dad has already planned our next adventure weekend. I can't wait!

Talk later,

Jaime

send

1 **Read the email. Mark ✓ the correct sentence.**

a Jaime had fun last weekend. ☐

b Jaime doesn't want another adventure weekend. ☐

c Jaime doesn't like paintballing. ☐

2 **Read the email again. Then, match and complete with *already*, *just*, or *yet*.**

1 The family

2 The Escape Center in town,

3 Jaime's dad

a hasn't opened _____.

b has _____ planned the next adventure weekend.

c has _____ gotten back from an adventure weekend.

Grammar: Present Perfect with *already, just, and yet*

We use *already* with the present perfect to talk about something that happened before.

We use *just* with the present perfect to talk about recently completed events.

We use *yet* with the present perfect to talk about things that haven't happened.

She has already finished reading her new book.

Pavlos has just baked a cake.

They haven't cleaned their room yet.

Remember!

We place *already* and *just* after *have* or *has* and before the verb.

They have already eaten their breakfast.

He has just written a new blog.

We place the word *yet* at the end of a negative sentence or question.

George hasn't arrived yet.

Have you seen the new movie yet?

3 Read the sentences and choose the correct words.

a Pete has **already** / yet had dinner.

b Jen hasn't finished her homework **just / yet**.

c Have they **already / yet** found the way out?

d Tim has **just / yet** repaired his bike.

e We haven't bought our new uniforms **yet / just**.

4 Complete the sentences with *already, just,* or *yet*.

a Niki has _____*already*_____ cleaned her room—she finished two hours ago.

b I have _____ finished playing soccer, and I am tired!

c Pat hasn't visited her cousins _____.

d Don't step on the floor! I've _____ mopped it!

e Have the children gone to bed _____?

5 Unscramble to make sentences using the present perfect.

a just / the tests / graded / our teacher
  Our teacher has just graded the tests.

b the new movie / yet / Helena and Marcus / not see
  _____

c visited / Omar / the doctor / already
  _____

d not open / yet / the presents / the children
  _____

e Mom / cooked / yet / dinner / ?
  _____

f already / play / the new video game / we
  _____

6 Look at the text and complete the sentences with the present perfect and *just*, *already*, or *yet*.

Cathy
finish homework at 7 p.m.

Ben and Fran
not go to the gym

Kylie
took a shower at 9:28 p.m.

Toni
did the dishes at 6 p.m.

The twins
not practice the piano

Grandpa
make a salad at 8 p.m.

It's 9:30 p.m.

a Cathy ___has already finished her homework___.

b Ben and Frank _____.

c Kylie _____.

d Toni _____.

e The twins _____.

f Grandpa _____.

7 Make true sentences about yourself. Use *already*, *just*, and *yet*.

a I have _____

b I haven't _____

c _____

also, too, either

We use *also* and *too* to give extra information.
We usually use *too* in informal sentences. *Too* usually goes at the end of a sentence, and we add a comma.

I like soccer, and I like swimming, *too*.

We use *also* before the main verb but after the verb *to be*.

He *also* **has to write a short story for school.**

I like painting, and I *also* **like drawing.**

They are *also* **interested in drama.**

We use *either* at the end of negative sentences.
We add a comma before *either*.

Simon doesn't enjoy surfing the Internet, and he doesn't like computer games, *either*.

1 **Read and choose the correct words.**

a   We didn't enjoy the movie or the book, **too / either**.

b   Gamal likes tennis and water polo, **either / too**.

c   Dina has visited China, and she has **too / also** visited Japan.

d   Amy doesn't go cycling or running, **also / either**.

e   She is **also / too** studying computer science.

f   Lee makes paper kites, and he makes board games, **too / also**.

2 **Complete the sentences with the correct words.**

> too   also   either

a   Rena doesn't like cheese. She doesn't like milk, _____.

b   Do they _____ like camping in the forest?

c   Xenia went to the park, and she went to Amy's, _____.

1 READ **Read the blog. Who did Tara see at the theater?**

THEATER WORLD

<u>a</u> Saturday, December 12

I have just had the best evening ever! Mom and I went to the theater to see my sister perform in a play.

___ The play was about a woman who saved a little girl. I really liked the costumes and the acting, too. However, we couldn't hear very well, and we couldn't understand a few things that happened, either. I knew what the story was about because I have also read the book. I think the book was better.

___ My sister's performance was very good. There were two people next to me, and they said that my sister was very good, too. They also said she should become a professional actress. I was really happy.

___ When the play ended, the spotlights focused on the two people next to me. I nearly fainted when I realized it was James Stiles and Monica Fox—my two favorite actors! They gave me their autographs, and we also took photos together.

___ I was so excited! I didn't expect that to happen, and Mom didn't, either.

2 EXPLORE **Label these features in the blog. Then, find and underline the sentences with *too*, *also*, or *either*.**

a day and date

b how Tara felt

c what happened at the play

d Tara's opinion

e what the play was about

3 PLAN Think about an interesting thing that happened to you. Then, complete the graphic organizer.

Title

_____

What happened?	What did you think?	How did you feel?
_____	_____	_____
_____	_____	_____

4 WRITE Write your blog. Use the graphic organizer to help you.

_____
_____
_____
_____
_____
_____
_____
_____
_____
_____
_____
_____
_____

CHECK

Did you ...
- write the day and date? ☐
- write your opinion? ☐
- write in the first person? ☐
- use *also*, *too*, and *either*? ☐

Look at the three pictures. Write about this story. Write 50 or more words.

_____

_____

_____

_____

_____

_____

Grammar: Present Perfect Questions with *How long*

HOW LONG HAVE THESE FOODS BEEN AROUND?

POPCORN

Some historians believe that the first popcorn came from Peru over 6,000 years ago! However, it is a fact that popcorn was important to the Aztec people of Mexico in the 1500s. The Spanish discovered popcorn in Mexico. They took it back to Spain. People have eaten popcorn for many years!

SANDWICHES

Some people believe that we have eaten sandwiches since 1762. In England, the Earl of Sandwich asked his cook to bring him something to eat while he sat playing cards. The cook brought him some meat between pieces of bread. The Earl liked it so much that, afterward, he ate it all the time. The aristocrats copied him and called this meal a *sandwich*.

ICE CREAM

There's chocolate, vanilla, strawberry, and so many more flavors! But how long have we eaten ice cream? Historians don't agree about the exact date. But we know that people ate frozen flavored milk in China almost 2,000 years ago!

1. **Read the poster. Are sandwiches older than ice cream?**

2. **Read the poster again. Then, complete the sentences.**

   a How long _____*have*_____ popcorn, sandwiches, and ice cream _____*been*_____ around?

   b People have eaten popcorn _____ many years!

   c The sandwich has been around _____ 1762.

We use the present perfect and *How long* to ask questions about an action that started in the past and is still happening.

> How long **have you had your new bike?**

> How long **have you lived in your home?**

Remember!

We answer using *for* or *since*.

> I've had my new bike **for** two weeks.

> We've lived in our home **since 2018.**

(3) Write the time expressions in the correct column.

> ~~three years~~   a year   last night   ~~yesterday~~
> a few months   2016   May   ten days   five weeks

Since	For
yesterday	three years
_____	_____
_____	_____
_____	_____

(4) Complete the questions using the correct form of the verbs. Then, circle the answers.

a   How long have you _____had_____ **(have)** your tablet? **For /** (**Since**) last year.

b   How long has she _____ **(know)** him? **For / Since** 1998.

c   How long has your teacher _____ **(work)** at your school? **For / Since** ten years.

d   How long have you _____ **(be)** at home today? **For / Since** two hours.

e   How long have sharks _____ **(exist)?** **For / Since** millions of years!

5 Look at the chart. Write questions with *How long* and answers with *for* or *since*.

Sara		two years		May
David		five years		six months
Sara and David		three years old		2014

a (Sara / skate) _How long has Sara skated? She has skated for two years._

b (David / play soccer) _____

_____

c (Sara and David / know each other) _____

_____

d (Sara / have her coat) _____

_____

e (David / be in Italy) _____

_____

f (Sara and David / live on the same street) _____

_____

6 Read and answer the questions about yourself.

a How long have you lived in your home?

_____

b How long have you known your best friend?

_____

TULIPS: A SHORT HISTORY

Tulips are beautiful flowers that have been popular for a long time. The Turkish people grew them first, hundreds of years ago.

Tulips have been an important part of Holland's history since the late 1500s. At first, they were simple, beautiful flowers. However, when someone named Carolus Clusius created many different colors, they became the most expensive flowers in Europe. Everyone wanted them!

Instead of money, people used tulip bulbs to buy things during the 1630s. They became popular in paintings and festivals, too. However, this didn't last for long.

Since then, people have continued to enjoy tulips, and Holland has continued to grow them. But they aren't as expensive now. That's great because Mom loves them!

---

1 **Read the text. Mark ✓ the correct word.**

Since the late 1500s, tulips have been very important in:

Turkey ☐   Holland ☐

2 **Read the text again and answer the questions.**

a How long have tulips been around? _____ For hundreds of years.

b What happened when Carolus Clusius created many different colors of tulips?

_____

c What did people in Holland use in the 1630s as money?

_____

d Has Holland continued to grow tulips?

Grammar: Present Perfect (*for/since*) vs. Past Simple

We use the present perfect to talk about events that started in the past and have just finished or are still happening.

Martin has played the guitar since he was five.

We use the past simple to talk about events that started and ended in the past.

Dora played the guitar an hour ago.
She lived in Paris last year.

Remember!

We usually use *for* and *since* with the present perfect.
We usually use *ago* and *yesterday* with the past simple.

I've been here since three o'clock.
I went to China three years ago.

(3) Write the time phrases in the correct column.

> since 2014   in 1981   last week   for three days
> two months ago   for five days   a few weeks ago
> since May   in December   since yesterday

Present Perfect	Past Simple
since 2014	in 1981

(4) Read the sentences. Write *PS* for past simple and *PP* for present perfect.

a Ahmad watered the flowers yesterday.   PS

b Helen has worn the same T-shirt for three days.   _____

c I walked to school last week because my bike broke.   _____

d Joe has missed the bus every day for three days in a row.   _____

e Gina ate all the cake yesterday.   _____

5 **Read and choose the correct words.**

a   I **went** / **have been** to the new store on Saturday morning.

b   Sandra **has owned** / **owned** a bike since last year.

c   My parents **have owned** / **owned** a restaurant six years ago.

d   Kim **hasn't gone** / **didn't go** to piano lessons since February.

e   Cassie **lived** / **has lived** in Los Angeles when she was six.

f   Zoe and Adam **haven't eaten** / **didn't eat** a pizza for more than three months.

6 **Look at the fact file and complete the sentences with the present perfect or past simple form of the verbs.**

Royal Tomb of Egypt

● Archeologists <u>discovered</u> (discover) a royal tomb in December 2018.

● The tomb _____ (be) in Sakkara, a city near Cairo, for more than 4,000 years.

● The archeologists _____ (find) 45 statues in the tomb.

● The royal family inside the tomb _____ (rule) in Egypt from 2500 BCE to 2350 BCE.

● Since February 2018, archeologists _____ (found) many other important ancient tombs.

● Tourists _____ (not see) the new tombs yet because archaeologists are still working on the sites.

A statue in a tomb, Egypt

7 **Make true sentences about yourself. Use *since*, *for*, *last week*, or *ago*.**

a   I have _____ since _____ .

b   I have _____ for _____ .

c   I _____ last week.

d   _____ ago.

Why / Why don't ... ? Because ...

We usually answer *why* questions with *because* to give a reason.

Why **did you buy a new watch?**

Because **my old one stopped working.**

We can also use *why* questions to make suggestions.

Why don't **you eat more fresh fruit? It's good for you!**

When we use *why don't* to make suggestions, we don't use *because* in the answer.

Why don't **we go for a walk?**

That's a good idea.

1 **Read and match.**

1	Why don't you buy the red hat?	a Because I'm having a party.
2	Why are you so sad?	b Because I didn't feel well.
3	Why did you buy so much ice cream?	c It looks good on you.
4	Why don't you go to practice earlier?	d Because I can't find my dog.
5	Why didn't you go to class today?	e You won't be late.

2 **Read and choose the correct options.**

1 Why are you learning English?
a Because I want to live in England one day. b It's amazing.

2 Why don't you buy your mom a necklace?
a Because she loves accessories. b She loves jewelry.

3 Why is Maxine late again?
a Because she missed the bus. b She will be here soon.

4 Why don't the children play outside?
a It's a beautiful day. b Because it's a beautiful day.

5 Why is your dad angry?
a It's not nice. b Because I lost his favorite book.

1 READ Read the brochure. What can you find out about dinosaurs?

The Nature Museum

Did you know that sharks are more than 400 million years old?

This week, The Nature Museum has a very interesting exhibition on sharks. Why visit it? Because there's lots of information on how they have survived for millions of years and how they have changed over time.

Are you interested in dinosaurs and how they lived? Why don't you visit the dinosaur bones we have brought in from Australia and Ireland? They are fascinating!

Why don't you come and find out what wiped out the dinosaurs and why they are now extinct?

Not interested in the past? Why don't you visit the Life in the Dark exhibition?

You will learn about all kinds of animals and insects that stay awake during the night!

Have you ever wondered about life in space? The new exhibition about life on Mars will answer all of your questions! The space exhibition also has ancient meteorites on display.

Why should you visit The Nature Museum? Because it's amazing!

Where to find us:
23 Richmond St, Mascot

Price:
Children $5, Adults $8

Hours:
Monday–Sunday
11 a.m.–7 p.m.

2 EXPLORE Mark ✓ the features that appear in the brochure. Then, underline the sentences that use *why* in red and *why don't* in green.

a   prices of tickets ☐

b   address ☐

c   hours ☐

d   what you can see and do there ☐

e   who you should visit the museum with ☐

f   why you should visit the museum ☐

g   what you can eat there ☐

3 **PLAN** Think about a museum or another place you like. Then, complete the graphic organizer.

One Thing You Can
See and Do There
_____
_____

Second Thing You
Can See and Do There
_____
_____

Name of Museum
_____

Why You Should Visit
the Museum
(Include *Why / Why
don't* and *Because*)
_____
_____

Address, Prices,
and Hours
_____
_____
_____

4 **WRITE** Write your brochure. Use the graphic organizer to help you.

_____
_____
_____
_____
_____
_____
_____
_____
_____

CHECK

Did you ...
- include the address? ☐
- include what you can do there? ☐
- include the price? ☐
- use *Why / Why don't?* and *Because*? ☐

Look at the picture and read the story. Then, complete the sentences about the story.

Ben's class went to the museum to learn about Ancient Egypt. They met outside the school at 9 a.m. and got on the bus at 10 a.m. The bus got to the museum at 10:30 a.m.

Mrs. Smith, their history teacher, told the children to be very quiet in the museum. She also told them not to touch anything. The museum was very interesting, and the children learned a lot about the history of Egypt and the mummies.

In one room, there was a big tomb. Ben decided to play a joke on the class. He hid behind the tomb, and when Mrs. Smith and a few children walked by, he made some strange noises. Penny got very scared and started running.

"Stop running!" shouted Mrs. Smith, but Penny didn't hear her. Penny fell down and knocked over a gold statue. The statue didn't break, but the museum guide was very angry. Penny started crying.

"I'm sorry," said Ben. "It was a joke."

"That's OK, Ben, but you must stay next to me all day now," said Mrs. Smith. Ben helped the museum guide lift the statue and clean it. The museum guide said Ben's joke was funny, but next time, Ben should play his jokes outside the museum.

Example Ben's class visited the museum to learn about Egyptian _____history_____.
They were on the bus for half _____an hour_____.

1   Mrs. Smith is Ben's _____.

2   The children weren't allowed to make noise or _____ anything
in the museum.

3   The children thought the museum was _____.

4   Ben made strange noises from _____ the tomb.

5   Penny got scared and started _____.

6   The museum guide was angry because a gold statue _____ on the floor.

7   Ben _____, but he had to stay next to Mrs. Smith all day.

6 Where does food come from?

✈ New Message

Dear Sonia,

I had the best time yesterday afternoon. We went to a farmers' market. It was amazing! All the food was delicious! Everything there was fresh and tasted so different from the produce that we usually buy in supermarkets.

I met someone named Julia. She showed us how to use leftover food to make new meals. That way, we don't waste anything. That's something we don't do enough. The best thing is that anyone can use her tips.

We tasted everything at the market, but no one bought anything because we'd already eaten too much!

Everyone in our family had a great time. No one complained, except for John. He didn't like anything at the market, not even the chocolate cake because it had honey instead of sugar.

Did you do anything interesting yesterday?

Write soon,

Cathy

1. **Read the email. Who didn't like anything at the farmers' market?**

2. **Read the email again. Underline the indefinite pronouns. Then, match.**

   1 Everything Cathy tasted   a complained about the market.

   2 No one bought anything   b was different from supermarket food.

   3 No one except for John   c because they had already eaten a lot.

We use indefinite pronouns to talk about people or things without saying who or what they are. They are formed with *every-*, *some-*, *any-*, or *no-*. We use pronouns ending in *-one* for people, and pronouns ending in *-thing* for things.

There is someone at the door.

There is no one here! Everyone is in the library.

There is something in the box.

Is there anything to eat?

There's nothing in the fridge.

Remember!

We often use *any-* pronouns in questions and negative statements.

Is there anyone in the classroom?

We don't have anything to do today.

No one is two words.

No one went to the party last night.

---

3 **Read and choose the correct words.**

a   I'm so bored. There's **something / nothing** to do!

b   José didn't eat **something / anything** for lunch.

c   The store is empty. There's **no one / someone** in it.

d   Do you know **anything / anyone** famous?

e   **Someone / Anyone** called my name in the crowd, but I couldn't see who.

f   **Everyone / Anyone** liked the party.

4 **Read and complete the sentences with the words from the box.**

a   Can you see _____anyone_____ in the room?

b   Ouch! There is _____ in my shoe!

c   Dad is sad because _____ wanted to go to the movie with him.

d   Don't say _____ to Sara about the surprise party!

e   _____ in my family is tall except me.

> ~~anyone~~
> anything
> everyone
> no one
> something

5 **Look and complete the sentences with words from the box.**

> nothing   ~~someone~~   everything   no one   anything

Someone
is in the room.

_____
you need to make the
cake is on the table.

The children didn't know
_____ about
the broken window.

There was
_____ at
the beach on Sunday.

There was
_____
in the cabinet.

6 **Unscramble the words to make sentences.**

a   nothing / there's / we / do / can / to / them / help

   There's nothing we can do to help them.

b   didn't / anything / Jane / buy / at the / market

   _____

c   enjoyed / the / play / everyone / we / performed in

   _____

7 **Read and complete the sentences about yourself.**

a   No one in my family is _____.

b   I don't know anyone who has _____.

c   Everything _____.

55

Evan: Guess what, Tomas! Dad found a cockroach in the kitchen. It was awesome!

Tomas: What? You didn't keep it, did you?

Evan: No, I didn't. We trapped it in a glass jar and took it outside to let it go.

Tomas: You aren't going to tell your mom, are you? She hates cockroaches!

Evan: I know. Then, guess what happened next!

Tomas: What?

Evan: I found a beautiful hairy spider in the backyard.

Tomas: Beautiful? They're ugly! You didn't trap it, too, did you?

Evan: Yes, I did. It's in a glass tank next to the snake tank. You want to come and see it, don't you?

Tomas: You're joking, aren't you? You know I don't like insects and spiders and …

Evan: Yes, I do. But I love them! I'm strange, aren't I?

Tomas: Yes, you are, Evan. But you're still my friend!

1 Read the dialogue. Then, mark ✓ the correct sentence.

a Evan keeps the cockroach. ☐

b Evan likes spiders. ☐

c Tomas loves insects. ☐

2 Read the dialogue again and complete the sentences.

> ~~did you~~   aren't I   are you

a **Tomas:** You didn't keep it, _____ did you _____?

b **Tomas:** You aren't going to tell your mom, _____?

c **Evan:** I'm strange, _____?

Grammar: Tag Questions

We use tag questions at the end of a short sentence to check information, emphasize a point, or ask if someone agrees with us.

She's good at science, isn't she?

John isn't playing tennis, is he?

They have studied insects for three years, haven't they?

I'm very tired, aren't I?

Remember!

We use a negative tag question when the sentence is in the affirmative.

    There are three people here, aren't there?

We use a positive tag question when the sentence is in the negative.

    They didn't see the new movie, did they?

(3) Read and match.

1 They don't want more food,

2 The swimming pool was closed,

3 We were having a good time,

4 It's a great movie,

5 I'm the team leader this week,

6 They didn't win the game,

a did they?

b aren't I?

c do they?

d weren't we?

e isn't it?

f wasn't it?

(4) Read and choose the correct words.

a They haven't seen the new movie yet, **have they** / **haven't they**?

b Joe has played tennis before, **has he / hasn't he**?

c Lisa doesn't enjoy her piano lessons, **does she / doesn't she**?

d Will and Graham were skiing yesterday, **were they / weren't they**?

e He's Italian, **isn't he / is he**?

f They had a sandwich for lunch, **didn't they / did they**?

5 Complete the sentences with tag questions.

a You have seen the doctor, _____ haven't you _____ ?

b I'm invited to the party, _____ ?

c There's someone in the room, _____ ?

d We don't have any ice cream, _____ ?

e Mom is working late, _____ ?

f You saw the puppy, _____ ?

6 Look and complete the sentences.

a She _____ is _____ in the park, isn't she?

b They _____ sad, aren't they?

c The dog _____ all morning, didn't he?

d There _____ any bread, is there?

e They _____ riding their bikes, aren't they?

f They _____ at the movie theater, were they?

7 Complete to make true sentences about you.

a I am _____, aren't I?

b My family is _____, _____?

c My teacher wasn't _____ last week, _____?

d My parents _____, _____?

e I don't have a _____, _____?

Improve Your Writing

Adjective Order

When we have more than one adjective in a sentence before a noun, we use a specific order.

1	2	3	4	5
opinion	size	physical description	age	color
amazing	small	tall	old	red

But we don't normally use five adjectives!

Jane bought some delicious big red **apples.**

1 **Read and complete to combine the sentences into one.**

a I have a jacket. It's old. It's blue.

I have an _____old blue jacket_____.

b Mary is eating a banana. It's yellow. It's delicious.

Mary is eating _____.

c There's a garden in the park. It's pretty. It's small.

There's a _____.

d They have a bird. It's big. It's black. It's strange.

They have a _____.

e Joe has an interesting book. It's big. It's old.

Joe has an _____.

f They bought a bike. It's nice. It's green. It's big.

They bought a _____.

2 **Read and write the adjectives in the correct order.**

a They have a _____large silver_____ cup. **(silver / large)**

b Where's my _____ backpack? **(green / new)**

c Elena has a _____ ring. **(small / beautiful / gold)**

d I had a _____ muffin for breakfast. **(big / chocolate)**

e Did you see any _____ elephants at the zoo?
(gray / huge / wonderful)

Writing: An Ad

1 READ Read the ad. Which location sells cupcakes?

JIM'S SMOOTHIES— DELIVERED TO YOUR DOOR!

Jim makes the most amazing smoothies in town!
Fresh, delicious, and cheap!
10% discount for students.

Contact Jim at 213-732-5718

Cupcakes can be healthy, can't they?

At Diane's Cake Bakery, we use all fresh ingredients from local farms. We make our cupcakes with a lot of vegetables and nutritious honey instead of sugar.

This week's special is a delicious light carrot cake—a tasty old recipe Diane has used for years.

Visit us at 20 Sunnymead Avenue!

2 EXPLORE Read the two ads again. Which ads include the items listed below? Write *D* for Diane's Cake Bakery or *J* for Jim's Café. Then, underline the slogans in the ads.

a a discount   _____

b an address   _____

c a slogan   _____

d adjectives in the correct order   _____

e a phone number   _____

3 **PLAN** Think about a product you like. Complete the graphic organizer. Then, draw your logo.

Product Name: _____

What is good about it?

_____

_____

_____

_____

What is your slogan?

_____

_____

_____

_____

Draw your logo.

4 **WRITE** Write your ad. Use the graphic organizer to help you.

_____

_____

_____

_____

_____

_____

_____

_____

_____

_____

_____

CHECK

Did you ...
- say what your product is? ☐
- use adjectives in the correct order? ☐
- write your slogan? ☐
- include a logo? ☐

Read and choose the correct words to complete the story.

orchard   livestock   pests   greenhouse   quarantine
imported   took   everything   anything   spoil

Last week, Enrique and his parents visited a farm. The first thing they did was walk through the beautiful big ___orchard___ . They picked some oranges and lemons and ate them. "I have never eaten delicious big oranges like these before," said Enrique.

Then, they helped with the **1** _____. They collected milk and eggs and took them over to the farmhouse. "We use these in our dairy products," said the farmer. "Here, have some cheese." Enrique's mom tasted the cheese. She loved it!

Next, they went into a large **2** _____. There were lots of vegetable plants in it. The farmer showed them a plant with big green leaves. "We **3** _____ this plant from Mexico. It's an avocado plant. We use it in salads and in other foods, too." They took some avocados and went into the kitchen.

With the farmer, they made a big dinner. **4** _____ was delicious. After dinner, Enrique and the farmer put all the leftovers in the fridge. "We never throw away our food. We put it in the fridge, so it doesn't **5** _____." Everyone had a good time at the farm. Enrique enjoyed it because he learned where all of the food comes from.

Mark ✓ the best name for the story.

Delicious Oranges ☐

A Tasty Meal ☐

A Visit to a Farm ☐

7 Why is water important?

Grammar: *Before/after/when/as* Clauses

HOW TO CONSERVE WATER

Why is water important? Because we can't live without it! We need water to drink, grow food, cook, and stay clean. And animals need it to survive, too. Water is a valuable resource. Here are some things that we can do every day to save water:

- As you are brushing your teeth, turn off the faucet.
- When you need to wash, take a quick shower instead of a bath.
- Before you wash the dishes after breakfast, think about it. It's best to do the whole day's dishes after dinner. That way, you conserve water by only washing them once a day. Do you have a dishwasher? Don't turn it on until after it's full.

- Don't throw out the water you use to hand wash your clothes. After you finish, you can use that water to wash your bike!

1. **Read the pamphlet. Why should we only do the dishes once a day?**

2. **Read and complete the sentences with *before*, *after*, *when*, or *as*.**

   a _____After_____ you finish washing your clothes by hand, you can use that water to wash your bike.

   b Take a quick shower _____ you want to wash yourself.

   c Make sure your dishwasher is full _____ you turn it on.

   d Turn off the faucet _____ you are brushing your teeth.

Grammar: *Before/after/when/as* Clauses

We use *before*, *after*, *when*, and *as* to join two parts of a sentence together.

Before cell phones, people used telephones.

Gary rode his bike after he finished his homework.

When they were having a water fight, it started raining.

Penny poured the liquid as Gary read the instructions.

Remember!

If the *before/after/as/when* part of the sentence comes first, we use a comma.

When I was sleeping, my dog started barking.

3 Read and choose the correct words.

a (**When**) / **Before** you come home, clean up the living room.

b **Before** / **After** I spoke to my teacher, I understood the activity.

c We were laughing **as** / **after** Frank was telling his silly jokes.

d Check that all the windows and doors are locked **after** / **before** you leave.

e We were shocked **when** / **after** we saw the burglar trying to open our front door.

f **After** / **Before** Ben watered the flowers, they looked much better.

g We listened carefully **as** / **after** the teacher explained the lesson.

4 Complete the sentences with words from the box.

> ~~after~~   before   when   after   as

a We can have ice cream _____ after _____ we have dinner.

b _____ the rollercoaster went downhill, we screamed.

c The boy was listening to music _____ he was repairing his bike.

d _____ John came home from school, he took a short nap.

e _____ we started the test, the teacher let us review our notes.

5) Look and complete the sentences.

Isabel washed her hands
_____before_____ she had
_____a sandwich_____ .

_____ Dario
played soccer, he took a
_____ .

_____ the
_____ jumped on the
table, it knocked over the vase.

_____
Wendy fell asleep, she read a
_____ .

6) Rewrite the sentences using the clauses in parentheses.

a The children watched TV. They had dinner. **(after)**

The children watched TV after they had dinner.

b We went on a camping trip. The school year started. **(before)**

_____

c Jane saw her old school friend. She was on her way to the gym. **(as)**

_____

d We always have a good time. We play with our friends. **(when)**

_____

7) Complete the sentences about yourself.

a I always _____ before _____ .

b After I have breakfast, I _____ .

c When I _____ , _____ .

I can't believe how many chores I had to do today! First, I had to take out the garbage for Mom, and I had to wash the dishes. Next, I had to sweep the driveway for Dad. Then, Magda, my older sister, said I had to help her clean the living room. I was already tired, but I still had to clean my own room because I always have to on Saturdays. I thought I was done then. But my brother and I had to rake up all the leaves in the yard. *And then,* I remembered that I had to start my school project. That was the hardest chore of all!

1 **Read the text. Then, mark ✓ the correct ending to the sentence.**

Jenna had to …

a   clean the kitchen.   ☐

b   wash the dishes.   ☐

c   cut the grass.   ☐

2 **Read the text again. Then, write three things that Jenna had to do. Use complete sentences.**

a   _____

b   _____

c   _____

Grammar: *Had to* (Obligation in the past)

We use *had to* to talk about obligations, or things we needed to do, in the past.

They had to wait for the bus for two hours.

Harry had to water the flowers.

Remember!

We form the negative with *didn't + have to + verb.*

Sarah didn't have to get up **early yesterday.**

We didn't have to go **to school last week.**

3 **Read and choose the correct words.**

a   Mary **had to /** (**didn't have to**) go to the doctor because she felt better.

b   We **had to / didn't have to** conserve water because it hadn't rained for months.

c   Emin **had to / didn't have to** go to soccer practice because he was sick.

d   They **had to / didn't have to** take a taxi because the bus was late.

e   Sue **had to / didn't have to** take an umbrella to school because it was raining.

f   Adan **had to / didn't have to** get up early during his vacation.

4 **Complete the sentences with *had to* or *didn't have to*.**

a   Jill _____had to_____ practice the piano every day when she was younger. ✓

b   We _____ stay inside because it was a nice day. ✗

c   Kerry and Mandy _____ take the exam yesterday. ✓

d   Dad was happy because he _____ go to work. ✗

e   My brother _____ walk to school because Dad drove him. ✗

f   Sandy _____ get a present for her sister's birthday. ✓

5 Read and unscramble to make sentences.

a   Kelly / read a book / English class / for her / had to

Kelly had to read a book for her English class.

b   Marco / go to the doctor / last week / didn't have to

_____

c   The girls / swim in the race / had to / in the cold weather

_____

d   We / buy bottled water / had to / for our trip

_____

e   Mr. Rowling / walk to school / had to / when he was young

_____

6 Look at the pictures. Then, make sentences with *had to* or *didn't have to* and the words in parentheses.

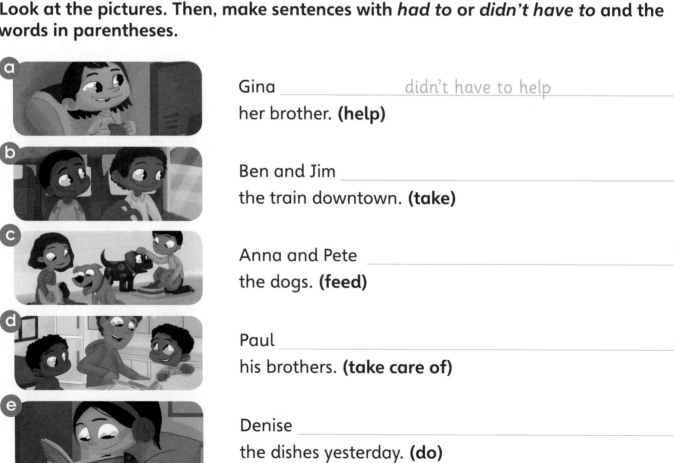

Gina _____ didn't have to help _____
her brother. **(help)**

Ben and Jim _____
the train downtown. **(take)**

Anna and Pete _____
the dogs. **(feed)**

Paul _____
his brothers. **(take care of)**

Denise _____
the dishes yesterday. **(do)**

Improve Your Writing

Verbs with Countable and Uncountable Nouns

When we talk about ingredients or equipment, we use countable and uncountable nouns.

some water

some glitter

a jar

Remember!

Most uncountable nouns do not have a plural form. We use *some* with uncountable nouns.

> **There is** some water **in the jar.**

We use *any* with questions and negative sentences.

> **Is there** any **glitter in the jar?**   **No, there** isn't any **glitter in the jar.**

1. **Read the sentences. Are the underlined nouns countable or uncountable? Write C for countable or U for uncountable.**

   a   There are three <u>glasses</u> on the shelf.   _C_

   b   You need some <u>sugar</u> for this experiment.   _____

   c   Where is the <u>milk</u>?   _____

   d   Do we have any <u>strawberries</u>?   _____

   e   There's some <u>soap</u> in the bathroom.   _____

   f   We don't have any <u>apples</u>.   _____

2. **Read and choose the correct words.**

   a   Is there **some /(any)** water in the bottle?

   b   There is **a / any** spoon on the table.

   c   We have **three / a** oranges in the basket.

   d   There is **a / some** honey in the jar.

   e   You need **some / a** glue for the experiment.

   f   Are there **some / any** children in the park.

1 READ Read the instructions. What household items can you use to make slime?

Homemade Slime

Materials:

▶ ½ cup of clear, thick shampoo

▶ some food coloring

▶ ½ cup of water

▶ a spoon

▶ a jar

▶ some glitter (optional)

What do you need to do?

1 Put the shampoo in a bowl and stir it slowly. Keep stirring until the shampoo is thick.

2 Add some food coloring. Add a drop at a time and mix well until you get the color you like.

3 Add some water. Stir it slowly so you don't make bubbles.

4 Then, add the rest of the water. Stir it slowly and stop when the mixture is very thick but still soft.

5 Add some glitter to make the slime sparkle. (optional)

6 Put the slime in a jar and cover it. Put the jar in the fridge for two days.

★ Stir the slime before you use it and put it back in the fridge after you finish playing with it.

2 EXPLORE Read the instructions again. Mark ✓ the features that the instructions have. Then, find and underline the uncountable nouns in the instructions.

a the number of steps ☐

b the name of the shampoo ☐

c a list of materials needed to make slime ☐

d a picture of the slime ☐

e an explanation of why this is a good way to make slime ☐

3 **PLAN** Think about something you can make using water, such as slime or a snow globe. Then, complete the graphic organizer.

Product: _____

Materials: _____

_____

_____

_____

Steps: _____

_____

_____

_____

Extra Information: _____

_____

4 **WRITE** Write the instructions to make your product. Use the graphic organizer to help you.

_____

_____

_____

_____

_____

_____

_____

_____

CHECK

Did you ...

- write the materials? ☐
- write the steps? ☐
- number the steps? ☐
- use countable and uncountable nouns? ☐

Look and read. Choose the correct words and write them on the lines. There is one example.

Example   A place with no water that we cannot use to grow plants.   _wasteland_

irrigation   valuable   blocked

deer

dirt

root

sink

1	We walk or drive on this to get from one side to the other.	_____
2	This is part of a plant under the earth that helps it live by collecting water.	_____
3	A period of heavy rain in India.	_____
4	Water comes out of this in our homes.	_____
5	A place with lots of water, mud, and marshes.	_____
6	This is in the kitchen, and we do the dishes in it.	_____
7	We can put things in this.	_____
8	This is when we water crops using pipes and canals.	_____
9	This stops water from flooding an area and also can collect and store water.	_____
10	A piece of land with lots of water around it.	_____

dam

swamp

island

bridge

faucet   **wasteland**   monsoon   container

8 How do numbers shape our lives?

Grammar: Verb + Gerund

Niko: Hi, Jake!

Jake: Hi, Niko. What are you doing this weekend?

Niko: I'm going to surf at the beach.

Jake: I love surfing. Do you remember surfing in Escondido last year?

Niko: Yeah, it was great. I'm surfing in a competition there next month.

Jake: Really? Can you imagine winning? That'd be awesome!

Niko: Yeah, it would be. Do you want to sign up, too? I recommend registering soon.

Jake: No, thanks! I love surfing, but I don't like competing. I like competing in math though.

Niko: I can't imagine competing in math. I definitely prefer surfing instead! I have to go! Bye.

Jake: See you soon!

1 **Read the dialogue. What does Jake like?**

2 **Read the dialogue again and circle the gerunds. Then, complete the sentences.**

a Jake loves _____surfing_____ .

b Jake doesn't like _____ .

c Jake asks Niko if he can imagine _____ .

d Niko recommends _____ for the competition soon.

Some verbs can be followed by a gerund. For example, *enjoy*, *like*, *recommend*, *imagine*, *suggest*, *avoid*, and *remember*. Remember, gerunds are nouns formed from a verb.

Paul loves playing dominoes.

Jenny enjoys giving her dog a bath. Her dog doesn't like getting a bath.

Gina and Frankie remember winning the geometry competition last year.

Remember!

We don't use two gerunds together. Instead, we use a gerund after a verb.

Incorrect: We enjoying swimming in the ocean.
Correct: We enjoy swimming in the ocean.

3) Read and match.

1 Sally enjoys

2 Dad doesn't like

3 We should avoid

4 Pete and Max love

5 Rena doesn't remember

6 The doctor suggested

a eating too much candy because it's bad for our health.

b meeting her aunt Julie a few years ago.

c rollerblading in the summer.

d exercising more to stay in shape.

e getting up early on Sunday mornings.

f swimming in the ocean. It's fun.

4) Complete the sentences with the gerund form of the words from the box.

a Can you imagine _____living_____ on Mars one day?

b Dennis doesn't like _____ the garbage out.

c Do you recommend _____ the new action movie?

d George started _____ his project a few hours ago.

e I don't mind _____ my grandparents with the housework.

do
help
~~live~~
see
take

5 Make sentences using the words in parentheses.

a Do _____you like listening_____ to music? **(you / like / listen)**

b _____ in the mountains. **(Ahmet / miss / live)**

c _____ cartoons in the morning before school.
(the children / love / watch)

d Can _____ a gold medal in the Olympics?
(can / you / imagine / win)

e _____ in the sun all day. **(Claire / not / enjoy / sit)**

6 Look and complete the sentences with the gerund form of the words in parentheses.

John loves
_____taking_____
bubble baths. **(take)**

The twins enjoy
_____
dinner. **(cook)**

The teacher suggested
_____ a
little harder. **(study)**

Ellen recommended
_____
The Animals Escape. **(buy)**

Mrs. Cook avoided
_____ on
the busy road. **(drive)**

7 Use gerunds to complete the sentences about yourself.

a I love _____ in the summer.

b I don't like _____ after school.

c I enjoy _____ .

Students of the Week Profiles

Shelly Richards

● wants to be an accountant because she loves working with numbers.

● plans to participate in the international math competition next winter.

● has decided to volunteer at the zoo this summer.

● needs to save money to buy a new laptop because her old one is very slow.

● prefers dancing to swimming.

● doesn't like to see homeless cats and dogs on the streets.

George Shaw

● doesn't want to study math because he wants to be an artist.

● is learning to speak Chinese, Polish, and Arabic because he loves languages.

● has offered to work at a summer camp this year.

● cannot decide what to buy with his allowance, so plans to save it.

● prefers playing chess to computer games.

● doesn't like to see garbage in the street.

1 **Read the text. Which student loves learning languages?**

_____

2 **Read the text again and circle the verbs in the infinitive form. Then, answer the questions.**

Who:

a   loves working with numbers?   _____Shelly_____

b   has offered to work this summer?   _____

c   wants to be an artist?   _____

d   doesn't like seeing homeless cats and dogs on the street?   _____

e   needs to buy a new laptop?   _____

Grammar: Verb + Infinitive

Some verbs can be followed by the infinitive form of another verb. For example, *agree*, *want*, *decide*, *need*, *plan*, *learn*, and *offer*.

Emma and Jane agreed to clean their room this weekend.

Paul decided to buy a comic book.

Some verbs can take the gerund or infinitive form of the verb. For example, *begin*, *like*, *love*, *prefer*, *try*, *start*, and *plan*.

Anna began playing the drums when she was six.

Anna began to play the violin when she was eight.

3 Sort the verbs depending on whether they can be used with a gerund, an infinitive, or both.

> agree   avoid   like   enjoy   decide   imagine   prefer   suggest   want

Gerund	Infinitive	Both

4 Complete the sentences using the infinitive form of the words from the box.

a   Jane wanted _____to make_____ a cake for her mom's birthday.

b   Harry prefers _____ healthy food instead of junk food.

c   The woman asked _____ the manager of the store.

d   George and Ann want _____ me this weekend.

> eat
> ~~make~~
> see
> visit

5 **Read and choose the correct words.**

a We plan **to play** / playing tennis on Sunday.

b Terry offered **giving / to give** me his old computer because mine broke.

c We decided **to learn / learning** Chinese last summer.

d Mom and Dad are planning **having / to have** a party this weekend.

e I don't mind **to help / helping** you this afternoon.

f Did the teachers suggest **to study / studying** a little harder?

6 **Read and make sentences using the gerund or the infinitive form of the verbs.**

a Kelly / want / buy / a new dress

Kelly wants to buy a new dress.

b the children / love / play / in the snow

c do / you / need / see / the doctor / this afternoon

d we / hope / visit / you / again / next summer

e Dr. Peters / recommends / walk / every day / for an hour

7 **Make true sentences about yourself using the verb + infinitive form.**

a I prefer _____.

b I want _____.

c I plan _____.

d I _____.

Although

We can use *although* at the beginning or in the middle of a sentence. It joins two different ideas together.

Although **there wasn't a lot of traffic, we were late for school.**

I enjoy watching soccer, although **I don't really understand the rules.**

Remember!

We use a comma to separate the two ideas.

Although **the weather was bad, we enjoyed our vacation.**

1 Read and match.

1 Although Tracy studied hard,

2 John enjoyed the trip to Chicago,

3 Although the children were tired,

4 Although I had a late dinner,

5 Laura helped her sister,

a they wanted to go to the park.

b although he didn't like the bus he traveled on.

c although she had very little time.

d she didn't pass the test.

e I was still hungry at bedtime.

2 Rewrite the sentences using *although*.

a I don't mind eating pasta tonight. I don't really like it.

I don't mind eating pasta tonight , although   I don't really like it   .

b We prefer traveling by train, but we don't like the frequent stops.

_____, although _____.

c They don't like working in the garden, but they love flowers.

Although _____.

d Math is my favorite subject, but I make a lot of mistakes in it.

_____, although _____.

e It was raining. We went to the park.

Although _____.

1 READ Read the letter. Why did Amir enjoy his math lesson yesterday?

12 Elm Street, Springfield

February 11

Dear Grandpa,

How are you? I had a really good time with you last month, although it's good to be home again.

You know that I don't like doing addition in math class, but I love drawing in art class. However, yesterday, my math class was amazing! Our teacher gave us a card with a number on it. We had to draw a shape that had as many sides as the number on the card. I got the number five. Although it was difficult at first, I drew a pyramid. This is because a pyramid has four triangle sides in it and a square at its base. So, that made five sides! Then, in art class, I drew a 3D version of my pyramid.

Now, every time I draw a shape, I think about what number represents that shape. This makes 3D shapes much easier to draw. I never thought numbers would help me in art!

What can you draw with the number six? Let me know!

Love,

Amir

2 EXPLORE Read the letter. Mark ✓ the features the letter has. Then, find and underline the sentences that use *although*.

a   an address ☐

b   a greeting using *Dear... ,* ☐

c   the date ☐

d   instructions ☐

e   a closing with *Love, ...* ☐

3 PLAN Think about something interesting you did at school or at home yesterday. Then, complete the graphic organizer.

Address _____

Date _____

Dear _____,

What did you do? _____

_____

Why did you enjoy it? _____

_____

Love, _____

4 WRITE Write your letter. Use the graphic organizer to help you.

_____

_____

_____

_____

_____

_____

_____

_____

CHECK

Did you ...

- write the address and date? ☐
- end with a closing? ☐

- start the letter with *Dear ...* , ☐
- use the word *although*? ☐

Look at the pictures. Write a story about what happens. Use at least 50 words.

_____

_____

_____

_____

_____

_____

_____

_____

_____

_____

_____

_____

What makes the natural world so amazing?

Grammar: Quantifiers

The Amazon Rainforest

- The Amazon rainforest covers many countries: Brazil, Bolivia, Peru, Ecuador, Colombia, Venezuela, Guyana, Suriname, and French Guiana. It has a lot of animals. It has over 1,300 bird species, 3,000 fish species, 430 mammals, and 2.5 million kinds of insects.

- It has over 40,000 plant species.

- There isn't much light on the floor of the rainforest because the top part of the trees is very thick.

- 20% of the world's oxygen comes from the Amazon.

- There are more than 400 indigenous groups that live in the Amazon, and a few of them have never made contact with people outside the forest.

- The Amazon has many dangerous animals that can attack you.

1 **Read the fact file. How many countries does the rainforest cover?**

2 **Read the fact file again and circle the quantifiers. Then, match.**

1 The Amazon has   a   oxygen comes from the Amazon.

2 A lot of the world's   b   a lot of animals and plants.

3 There are many   c   dangerous animals in the Amazon.

4 The trees are so thick that there   d   indigenous groups in the Amazon.

5 There are more than 400   e   isn't much light in the rainforest.

We use quantifiers to talk about amounts of things.
We use *many* and *a few* with countable nouns.

There were many beautiful butterflies in the tree.

Jim found a few dinosaur bones in the backyard.

We use *much* and *little* to talk about uncountable nouns.
We can use *a lot* of and *any* to talk about both countable and uncountable nouns.

There's very little chocolate milk in the bottle. There isn't much.

There are a lot of eggs, and there is a lot of orange juice in the fridge. There aren't any potatoes, and there isn't any bread.

Remember!

We use *any* in negative sentences and with questions.

We don't have any time to go swimming this weekend.

Do you have any cookies in your lunchbox?

3 **Read and circle the correct words.**

a Lisa has **a lot of** / **much** homework today.

b Mom sometimes eats **a few / much** chocolates after dinner.

c There are **much / many** children in the classroom.

d There's **very little / a few** time left to finish your homework.

e Are there **very little / any** people waiting for the bus tonight?

4 **Complete the sentences with the correct form of the words in the box.**

a There has been _____a lot of_____ rain this winter.

b Denise has _____ friends in Ankara she wants to visit.

c Do you have _____ time to go to the movies?

d How _____ skateboards does Stella have?

a lot of
any
a few
many

5 Look at the pictures and complete the sentences with *a lot of, any, a few, little, many,* or *much.*

There are
___a lot of___
bubbles in the air.

Jenny has too
_____ things to
do today.

There is very
_____ rain
falling.

There are _____
books on the shelf.

The children are making too
_____ noise.

There aren't
_____ cookies
in the cookie jar.

6 Unscramble and write the sentences.

a life / any / scientists / found / haven't / other / planets / on / yet

___Scientists haven't found any life on other planets yet.___

b was / a lot of / there / garbage / in / river / the

_____

c people / enjoy / many / listening / to / music

_____

d is / little / food / there / left / in / kitchen / the

_____

7 Complete the sentences about yourself.

a I have a few _____.

b I don't have any _____.

c There are many _____ in my neighborhood.

New Message ✕

Hi Susana!

I'm doing a project for our science class about David Attenborough. He's a person who I admire a lot. Let me tell you a little about him.

He's one of the most famous naturalists in the world. That means he's a person who studies nature.

He grew up near the University of Leicester, where his father was president. When he was 11 years old, he collected newts that came from a nearby pond. Then, he sold them to the university!

He travels all around the world. He goes to really cool places where he studies the plants and animals. And, he hosts many shows that are about the plants and animals that he studies. His shows are awesome. They have won many awards!

There are more than ten plants and animals that are named after him. Guess what? One of the plants eats rats!

I present my project tomorrow.
Wish me luck!

Pedro

🗑 | ▾

---

1 **Read the email. What does David Attenborough do?**

_____

2 **Read the email again. Then, complete the sentences using relative pronouns.**

a A naturalist is a person _____who_____ studies nature.

b The University of Leicester is _____ his father was the president.

c There are more than ten plants and animals _____ are named after him.

d He goes to really cool places _____ he studies plants and animals.

e He hosts shows _____ are about plants and animals.

Grammar: Relative Pronouns

Relative pronouns introduce clauses that give us extra information. We use *who* for people, *that* for things, and *where* for places.

Alexander Fleming is the man who discovered penicillin.

Roses are the flowers that my mom likes the best.

Now I live in Sydney, Australia, where I was born.

Remember!

We use a comma when the clause beginning with the relative pronoun is not needed for the main clause to make sense.

Jason is the boy in the red hat, who wants to be a doctor.

3 Read and circle the correct words.

a   That's the girl **where / who** sits next to me in class.

b   That's the place **who / where** she visits every week.

c   Are those the books **who / that** you borrowed last week?

d   We always help the old woman **where / who** lives on our street.

e   Is that the town **that / where** your dad was born?

f   We have two computers **who / that** don't work.

4 Complete the sentences with *who*, *where*, or *that*.

a   Jane bought a coat _____that_____ she really liked.

b   Helen likes movies _____ make her laugh.

c   That's the girl _____ I play soccer with.

d   The downtown stadium is _____ we practice every day.

e   This is the person _____ helped me find my lost dog.

f   That's the restaurant _____ we ate lunch.

5 Use the prompts to make sentences. Use *who*, *where*, or *that*.

a _____ That's the house where _____ my teacher lives.
(that's / house)

b _____ belongs to our neighbor.
(we / found / the cat)

c _____ was in her favorite movie.
(she / met / the actor)

d _____ my mom and dad met.
(that's / place)

e _____ _____ my brother made for lunch.
(I / don't like / the sandwiches)

6 Make sentences with *who*, *where*, or *that*.

a Sally is the piano teacher. Everyone likes her.

   Sally is the piano teacher who everyone likes. _____

b This is the school. I studied English.

   _____

c Fiona has a house. It's bigger than mine.

   _____

d Anna and Alex are the children. They broke the window.

   _____

e He owns a phone. It's is very expensive.

   _____

7 Make true sentences about yourself. Use *who*, *where*, or *that*.

a My home is a place _____.

b My mom is a person _____.

c _____ a hobby _____ I like a lot.

Stative Verbs

We usually use stative verbs to talk about permanent situations or a state that lasts for a while. We don't usually use stative verbs in the progressive form.

Gina is eating the apple. (action verb)
It tastes amazing. (stative verb)

We sometimes use stative verbs to describe temporary situations such as thoughts, opinions, and feelings.

Mark feels sad today. (stative verb)

1 **Read the sentences and write *S* for stative verb and *A* for action verb.**

a   Tracy likes science class. _____S_____

b   We bought three boxes of paper. _____

c   They are throwing a party on Saturday. _____

d   What does Kim think about the show? _____

e   We don't understand this lesson. _____

f   His idea sounds great. _____

2 **Read and circle the correct form of the verbs.**

a   The flower (smells) / is smelling amazing!

b   **Does Zoe have / Is Zoe having** any brothers?

c   I **am not thinking / don't think** fish are smart animals.

d   We **are liking / like** the Egyptian exhibition.

e   He **has / is having** two pet dogs.

f   They **have / are having** a brand-new car.

Writing: A Descriptive Paragraph

1 READ Read the descriptive paragraph. Can these animals see well?

Frogs are amphibians. Amphibians live on land and in water. But they can't live away from water because they will dry up and die. Water soaks through frogs' skin when they swim. This is why they don't have to drink water. It's also why their skin looks moist. Frogs also need water to lay their eggs. They breathe through their noses and skin, and they catch food with their tongues. They eat insects, worms, snails, and slugs. Large frogs also eat snakes and mice. When they eat, frogs push their eyeballs down to help them swallow the food. They have 360-degree vision. This means that they can see everything around them. Did you know that a group of frogs is called an army?

2 EXPLORE Read the descriptive paragraph again. Mark ✓ the features that it has. Then, find and underline the sentences that use stative verbs.

a information about what the animal looks like ☐

b information about what the animal eats ☐

c the writer's opinion about the animal ☐

d unusual facts about the animal ☐

e a closing with *Love, Bye, Thank you,* etc. ☐

3 PLAN Think about an animal you like. Then, complete the graphic organizer.

What does it look like?

_____

_____

Animal:

_____

Where does it live?

_____

_____

What does it eat?

_____

_____

What is unusual about it?

_____

_____

4 WRITE Now write your descriptive paragraph. Use the graphic organizer to help you.

_____

_____

_____

_____

_____

_____

_____

_____

_____

_____

_____

CHECK

Did you ...
- write what it looks like? ☐ • write where it lives? ☐ • write what it eats? ☐
- write what is unusual about it? ☐ • use stative verbs? ☐

Read the diary and write the missing words. Write one word on each line.

Example My dad is a paleontologist, and today my friend and I _____are_____ with him at work.

1 We are outside. Today he found _____ dinosaur bones.
They are very big. Our teacher taught us about dinosaurs in our history

2 _____ and showed us some pictures. The T-Rex was bigger

3 _____ other animals, and it was very dangerous, too. However, most dinosaurs were only as big as humans or smaller. Some dinosaurs only

4 _____ meat and some only ate plants.

5 They _____ on Earth for more than 160 million years. The only animal bigger than a dinosaur is the blue whale. Whales are mammals, but dinosaurs were reptiles and laid eggs.

Read the email. Choose the right words and write them in the blanks.

×

Hi Estefania,

What have you been up to?

I'm sooooo embarrassed. While I was riding my bike to school, it **0** <u>started</u> to rain.
It was **1** _____ than I've ever seen it here! I stopped to put on my raincoat—you know,
2 _____ pretty one that has polka dots? Jaime saw and came over to hold my bike for
me. But I told him I could do it **3** _____. He looked really surprised **4** _____
I sounded. "Calm down," he said. "If you hurry, you **5** _____ to school on time." I felt
soooo bad! He was just trying to be helpful. Have you **6** _____ done anything like that?
I **7** _____ to be so rude. I **8** _____ to be really friendly. I guess I was just
9 _____, but now I feel really angry at myself. I need to apologize to him!

If you **10** _____ any advice, you'll tell me, right?

Aneta

SEND

Example	start	(started)	starting
1	rainy	rain	rainier
2	a	an	the
3	himself	myself	itself
4	at how	by how	with how
5	getting	will get	won't get
6	ever	never	no
7	didn't used	didn't use	never use
8	used	use	never use
9	happy	angry	nervous
10	haven't	had	have

Read and choose the correct words to complete the ad.

DO YOU KNOW A PICKY EATER?

FUN FOODS

Fun Foods is the place for you! We have **0** _____just_____ opened the first ever restaurant designed especially for picky kids.

We all know **1** _____ who doesn't like vegetables and doesn't like fruit **2** _____, right? Well, our food is so much fun, kids like eating things they usually don't like.

Have you **3** _____ heard of pineapple-pea popsicles? They're frozen in the shape of a T. Rex. Look—they're super cool, **4** _____? How long has it been **5** _____ you had beet and hibiscus juice? Probably too long! Sip it through a silly straw. We even have a mummy meatloaf made of turkey. Our customers really love our rainbow fruit kebabs,

6 _____. And you can end your meal with avocado-cocoa volcano cake. It's amazing!

We **7** _____ using delicious fresh ingredients since we opened. And we are always making hundreds of **8** _____ combinations. Why **9** _____ try Fun Foods today? **10** _____ you'll love it!

24 Memory Lane   www.funfoods.com   473-223-2233

Example	yet	(just)	still
1	anyone	no one	someone
2	either	neither	too
3	yet	ever	never
4	isn't it	aren't you	aren't they
5	for	since	yet
6	either	neither	too
7	have been	has been	had been
8	new twelve	tasty new	new big
9	not you	don't they	don't you
10	While	Because	Just

Read and choose the correct words to complete the letter.

June 29

Dear Mom,

I thought you might like a letter while you're away on business.

You know I really enjoy **0** _making_ things. So I wanted to make a model of the solar system for science class. But no one else in the group could imagine **1** _____ one. Everyone else wanted to do an experiment instead. **2** _____ I didn't really want to, I agreed to help. We decided **3** _____ what a volcano looks like. I didn't have any idea how to do the experiment. We didn't have **4** _____ information about it either. But Mark did some research. He's the student **5** _____ always knows how to figure things out.

First, we **6** _____ get the supplies. We needed a rectangular container, a lemon, some vinegar, some baking soda, some food coloring, and some glitter. Then, we cut the lemon in half and put it in the container. Next, we cut off the tip of the lemon, and Juan poked it with his pencil several times. Miguel added **7** _____ drops of red and yellow food coloring and some gold glitter. Julieta added **8** _____ baking soda, and it started to foam. And, **9** _____ I poured the vinegar in, it really bubbled up and spilled glittery foam all over my new shoes!

It was cool. But, I definitely plan **10** _____ something different next time.

Love, Chelsea

Example	(making)	make	made
1	build	building	to build
2	Because	Although	When
3	to show	show	showing
4	much	no	some
5	where	when	who
6	must to	have to	had to
7	any	a few	much
8	some	one	a
9	where	when	who
10	make	making	to make

Acknowledgments

The authors and publishers acknowledge the following sources of copyright material and are grateful for the permissions granted. While every effort has been made, it has not always been possible to identify the sources of all the material used or to trace all copyright holders. If any omissions are brought to our notice, we will be happy to include the appropriate acknowledgments on reprinting and in the next update to the digital edition, as applicable.

Key: U = Unit.

Photography

All the photos are sourced from Getty Images.

UI: manonallard/E+; PhotoAlto/Belen Majdalani/PhotoAlto Agency RF Collections; aldomurillo/E+; STOCK4B/Getty Images Plus; Just John Photography/Moment; kali9/E+; **U2:** Juanmonino/E+; Colin Anderson Productions pty ltd/DigitalVision; SDI Productions/E+; 3DSculptor/iStock; Stocktrek/Photodisc; SCIEPRO/Science Photo Library; Steven Hobbs/Stocktrek Images; Yustinus/RooM; Anton Petrus/Moment; prescott09/iStock Editorial; **U3:** Maskot; JGI/Tom Grill; Fuse/Corbis; Prasit photo; desifoto/DigitalVision Vectors; aunaauna/iStock; Westend6I; Clarissa Leahy/DigitalVision; Highwaystarz-Photography/iStock; **U4:** Nophamon Yanyapong/EyeEm; Patrick Kunkel/ MITO images; Hero Images; aunaauna/iStock; Ariel Skelley/DigitalVision; **U5:** tataks/iStock; FuatKose/E+; Copyright Xinzheng. All Rights Reserved/ Moment; Daniel Bosworth/British Tourist Authority; Mario Ramadan/EyeEm; Glowimages; wildestanimal/Moment; **U6:** Jodie Griggs/Moment Mobile; Straitel/ iStock; Westend6I; up close with nature/Moment Open; mikroman6/Moment; Photographer Kris Krüg/Moment; **U7:** nicolas_/E+; Hero Images; Matthew Davidson/EyeEm; Laurent Hamels/PhotoAlto Agency RF Collections; Dave King/ Dorling Kindersley; dmitriymoroz/iStock; MamiGibbs/Moment; ArtLana; **U8:** PeopleImages/E+; South_agency/E+; VikramRaghuvanshi/E+; totallyout/iStock/ Getty Images Plus; **U9:** Global_Pics/E+; Slow Images/Photographer's Choice/ Getty Images Plus; Max Mumby/Indigo/Getty Images Entertainment; Chris Ware/Stringer/Hulton Archive; PicLeidenschaft/iStock; Craig P. Jewell/Moment; Sam Edwards/OJO Images; The Catcher Photography/Moment Open; Elke Sagray/EyeEm.

Illustrations

Illustrations by Collaborate Agency.
Cover illustrations by Alessia Trunfio (Astound).